Catholic Update
guide to
The Bible

MARY CAROL KENDZIA,
Series Editor

Franciscan
MEDIA
Cincinnati, Ohio

RESCRIPT

In accord with the *Code of Canon Law*, I hereby grant my *Imprimatur*
the *Catholic Update Guide to the Bible*.

Vicar General and Auxiliary Bishop
of the Archdiocese of Cincinnati
Cincinnati, Ohio
October 30, 2012

The *Imprimatur* ("Permission to Publish") is a declaration that a book or pamphlet is considered
to be free from doctrinal or moral error. It is not implied that those who have granted the
Imprimatur agree with the contents, opinions or statements expressed.

Cover and book design by Mark Sullivan
Cover image © Fotolia | Mele Stemmermann

ISBN 978-1-61636-580-6

Printed in the United States of America.
Printed on acid-free paper.
13 14 15 16 17   5 4 3 2 1

Contents

About This Series

The Catholic Update guides take the best material from our best-selling newsletters and videos to bring you up-to-the-minute resources for your faith. Topically arranged for these books, the words you'll find in these pages are the same clear, concise, authoritative information you've come to expect from the nation's most trusted faith formation series. Plus, we've designed this series with a practical focus—giving the "what," "why," and "how to" for the people in the pews.

The series takes the topics most relevant to parish life—e.g., the Mass, sacraments, Scripture, the liturgical year—and draws them out in a fresh and straightforward way. The books can be read by individuals or used in a study group. They are an invaluable resource for sacramental preparation, RCIA participants, faith formation, and liturgical ministry training, and are a great tool for everyday Catholics who want to brush up on the basics.

The content for the series comes from noted authors such as Thomas Richstatter, O.F.M., Lawrence Mick, Leonard Foley, O.F.M., Carol Luebering, William H. Shannon, and others. Their theology and approach is grounded in Catholic practice and tradition, while mindful of current Church practice and teaching. We blend each author's style and approach into a voice that is clear, unified, and eminently readable.

Enrich your knowledge and practice of the Catholic faith with the helpful topics in the Catholic Update Guide series.

Mary Carol Kendzia
Series Editor

Introduction

Catholics today are seeking Jesus in the Scriptures as never before.

Many grew up in an era when the Church, busy doing other things, was not putting much energy into teaching the Bible. Some Catholics even picked up a kind of fear of Bible reading—as if the danger of false interpretation was so great that it was better to have nothing to do with the Bible at all or that a father would give his children a gift so dangerous it could not be used.

Today, there is a new emphasis on Scripture among Catholics. Bible-study groups, an expanded emphasis on Scripture in the liturgy since the Second Vatican Council and encouragement from Church leaders has led many Catholics to dust off the family Bible, looking for nourishment for the spiritual life.

Unfortunately, many new students of Scripture quickly experience frustration and confusion. This need not happen if one starts with a solid introduction on how to approach the Bible.

Author Virginia Smith, who has written about Scripture, notes that when she first picked up her Bible she had just plunged in, assuming she was about to read a book cover to cover, unaware that she was actually entering a library where not one, but seventy-three books awaited her: books of poetry, books of song, letters, allegories, historical sagas, and more.

She reports sailing blandly along treating them all alike under the impression that, no matter where you open it, the Bible is the Bible is the Bible. She learned that there are better ways to approach the Bible and how to avoid that kind of pitfall.

What became obvious to her later was, without a lot of extra effort, she could have saved herself a lot of confusion.

The *Catholic Update Guide to the Bible* offers a brief journey through this "library" of sacred writings, a door through which we can begin to become acquainted with and grasp the immense wealth of inspired literature, and a connection to God's own Word.

Through building familiarity with the Bible, we feel more at home in this library. It is easier to find our way around, easier to move from one place to the other as we see how each book relates to other books, easier to access its richness.

It is a journey that can have a profound effect on our spiritual, emotional, relational, and physical well-being and health.

CHAPTER ONE

What Is the Bible?

Two basic principles should guide us each time we pick up the Bible: (1) The Bible is both the Word of God and the words of human beings. (2) The Bible is not a book—it is a library.

The Bible Is Divine *and* Human

First, the Bible is at the same time both the Word of God and the words of human beings. We have the same problem understanding the Bible as we have understanding Jesus. We believe that he is at once both fully human and fully divine. It is a mystery we cannot totally comprehend.

The Bible, too, is at the same time divine and human. It is truly God's Word, and when we read it prayerfully we experience its power to bring us into contact with the Lord. Yet it is embarrassingly human. The human authors show a woeful ignorance of science, history, and even theology, because God uses as authors human beings with all their limitations.

The authors of Genesis knew nothing of what modern science has discovered about the solar system. To that writer, the earth was a flat disk and the sky a solid dome, like a bowl turned upside down over a saucer. Above the bowl was a great ocean. The dome, or "firmament," had windows which the Lord could open at will to allow some of the water stored above to come down in the form of rain.

God did not free the inspired author from the scientific ignorance shared with the people of that time; God simply used those inaccurate ideas to get across his own message: that he had created everything that exists. So Genesis tells us that God created the firmament, and the Psalms tell us that he opens the windows when he chooses to send rain. The person of faith, as he or she reads, must sort out the human from the divine in the Bible.

Unfortunately, the sorting is not always quite as easy as in this example. Fortunately, each reader does not have to do the sorting alone, because we receive help from the Church: both from official statements and from the writings of the many women and men of faith who have made the study of the Bible their life's work.

The Bible Is a Library

The second principle we need to remember in reading the Bible is that this is not really a book; it is a library. Like the books on the typical library shelf, the seventy three books of the Bible have been written at various dates over a period of a thousand years, and in a variety of literary forms.

We notice great differences between ideas contained in one book of the Bible and another. Psalm 30 clearly denies that human beings can experience happiness after death; the later books of Daniel and Maccabees do speak of life after death. The book of Deuteronomy permits divorce; the prophet Malachi says that God detests it; Jesus calls remarriage after divorce adultery. Many other contradictions could be listed. This is because the Bible, like any library, gathers books written at various stages in the ongoing process of human development.

God's relationship with his people, like every human relationship, is a developing relationship. He reveals himself and his will gradually to his people, trying not to overwhelm them at any point with more truth than they can handle. He takes us where we are, and leads us toward fuller truth.

The Bible's Composition

Forty-six of the books form the Old Testament, which has as its unifying theme the covenant made between God and Moses on

Mount Sinai. The remaining twenty-seven books make up the New Testament, which focuses on the saving event of Jesus Christ. The original languages of the Old Testament are Hebrew, Aramaic, and Greek; the New Testament was composed in Greek.

The first eleven chapters of Genesis are a prehistory, a kind of verbal sketch relating, in story form, some of the basic beliefs of Israel's religion. Genesis 12 begins a historical account of Israel's origins, but a history heavily laced with folklore and family traditions. In succeeding books, we find not only history but also legal codes, oracles, prophetic sayings, hymns, psalms, lyrical poetry, biography, creeds, legends, proverbs, myths, letters, and Gospels. Through each book and literary form the biblical authors have expressed their understanding of God and the truths of their faith.

The Bible was not composed to teach science, catalog historical facts, or prophesy the rise and fall of America. It is above all a book of faith. A group of people recognized God's presence in their community, recorded their experiences over several centuries, and eventually collected and edited those traditions into the one volume we call the Bible. Through the pages of this sacred collection modern believers continue to experience the Lord whose loving presence has been a constant throughout all of salvation history.

Finding Your Way Through the Library

Every time we take the Bible down from the shelf, we fall into a faulty way of thinking that goes something like this: "It looks like a book. It feels like a book. Therefore, the Bible is a book." The reason we leap so readily to this conclusion is that the Bible, as we know it today, appears neatly bound between two covers, but that has not always been the case.

Originally, the manuscripts which would ultimately make up the Bible were painstakingly inked onto long and sometimes cumbersome scrolls of parchment or papyrus. Much later, in medieval times, the sacred Scriptures were equally painstakingly hand copied in monastery scriptoriums all over Europe. It was crystal clear to our predecessors in the faith that they were dealing, not with a book, but with many books. So the Bible is actually not a book at all; it is, rather, a collection of books or a little library.

When we visit a secular library, we don't expect all of the books to have been written during the same time frame. The same holds true for the Bible. Because we believe the Bible is inspired by God, we may be tempted to think it was published all at once and even picture it as having dropped from heaven, leather bound and gilt-edged, with chapter and verse numbers in place. In actuality, the Bible was written in different stages by authors who may have had no idea they were inspired by God or that they were writing for a time and place other than their own.

The earliest Old Testament accounts, those found in the books of Genesis through Deuteronomy (the Pentateuch or Torah), were preserved through long generations by word of mouth—oral tradition—and did not begin to take written form until about the tenth century B.C. The writing that would eventually make up the Bible then went on spasmodically through all the intervening years down to the latter part of the first century A.D. or even, possibly, into the second century A.D.

Yet, even among books written in a certain form, a library contains different takes on the same subject. All four Gospels have the same general purpose, of course. But each Gospel has its own style and flavor because four different authors and traditions were at work. Mark, for instance, concentrates on what Jesus did rather than on what he said, and on his suffering humanness rather than his divinity. Matthew is the Christian rabbi intent on catechesis. Luke has an eye for Jesus's mercy, for Christian prayer and renunciation, and for the poor. John presents a majestic, divine Jesus, and a kingdom of salvation already in force.

Questions for Reflection

1. How is the Bible organized?
2. Describe how the Bible is both divine and most human.
3. In what way is the Bible like a library?

CHAPTER TWO

The Old Testament

As a rule, we think of the Bible in terms of its two principal divisions, the Hebrew Scriptures and the Christian Scriptures, traditionally known as the Old Testament and New Testament.

Testament is not a word that crops up that often in everyday conversation, so perhaps it doesn't convey much to us. A better choice might be *covenant*, which can be defined as a solemn agreement between two parties. In the Scriptures, the parties involved are nearly always God and God's people. The importance of the word *covenant* is indicated by the fact that it appears 289 times in the *New American Bible*. From Genesis to Revelation, the idea of covenant is the golden thread weaving in and out through the Bible's many books.

7

From the first inkling of the covenant theme in the story of Noah (Genesis 9:9–17), we see that God has no interest in a race of robots, preprogrammed creatures who will obey him mechanically. God wants his people to choose him freely, serve him without coercion, and love him with open hearts.

This is why he chooses to enter into a covenant relationship with humankind. The covenant is first of all God's gift of love to us. We can enter a covenant with God only because God lovingly and freely offers it to us. Such a covenant was implied at the very creation of the human race. We, in turn, are invited and enabled to respond lovingly and freely to God's offer. Thus a covenant cannot be imposed; it must be freely accepted by both parties.

God's proposal of such an agreement, together with his people's acceptance and subsequent attempt to live it, forms the golden thread which binds all of salvation history together—Old Testament and New, 2000 B.C. and 100 A.D.—and which is found wherever the chosen people's travels may take them.

Remembering this notion of covenant is key in understanding the Old Testament: beginning with the Pentateuch (Greek for *five rolls* or *books*), also known as the Torah (Hebrew for *the Law*), and then proceeding to the Historical Books, the Wisdom Books (or The Writings), and then the Prophetic Books.

Pentateuch

The Greek prefix *penta* means "five" (as in the Pentagon in Washington, D.C.), so we are not surprised to find five books in this set: Genesis, Exodus, Leviticus, Numbers, and Deuteronomy. These works are the heart of the Hebrew Scriptures and the most treasured traditions of Judaism.

Genesis: The beginnings. In the Pentateuch, we discover the very earliest memories in the Judeo-Christian era. The first chapters and verses of Genesis (1:1—11:26) contain stories so old they are subtitled "Primeval" or "Prehistory," referring to that period predating written records and where the verification of certain episodes (such as the creation, the flood, the Tower of Babel) is difficult if not impossible to establish. The tales told in these first Genesis chapters found their way by word of mouth from generation to generation for a very long time before being committed to writing. As Catholics, we do not take the prehistorical chapters of Genesis (chapters 1—11) as literal history.

Since final work on the Pentateuch's written version wasn't completed until the sixth century B.C., it was difficult to reconcile divergent accounts of a specific episode into one. As a result, Genesis sets side-by-side two creation stories (1:1—2:4a, 2:4b—3:24) and merges two flood epics, one which speaks of saving two of every species (6:19) and one which calls for rescuing seven pairs (7:2–3). Though we do not take these prehistoric accounts literally, we believe they richly convey God's truth.

After the initial chapters of Genesis, it is as though the curtain has fallen on the prologue to the biblical drama and risen on the Age of the Patriarchs, an era which probably began in about the nineteenth century B.C.

A patriarch was a father figure for an extended family or clan which included a multitude of servants or slaves needed to tend large herds and flocks. The constant need to feed and water these animals made life in the patriarchal system nomadic.

The first historical biblical figure we meet is the leader of one of these family units. His name is Abram, later Abraham, and it is with him that the covenant relationship with God begins. The remainder of the book of Genesis deals with the four generations of patriarchs: Abraham, Isaac, Esau, and Jacob (later called Israel) and the twelve sons of Jacob, progenitors of the tribes of Israel. The focus is on Jacob's favorite son, Joseph, through the latter part of this book. As Genesis ends, Joseph, together with his father, brothers and assorted relatives, are living a life of ease and comfort in Egypt's Land of Goshen.

Exodus: Enter Cecil B. DeMille. Between the last lines of Genesis and the opening of the next book, Exodus, four centuries disappear and the situation of Jacob's descendants is radically different. Now called Israelites because all are from the line of Israel (Jacob), these Hebrew people are considered a threat to Egypt's security and are virtually enslaved. In terms of its ongoing significance, the book of Exodus is one of the most important in the Hebrew Scriptures.

Exodus means "departure," and, after crossing the Red Sea, it's off into the desert for the Israelites. The high point of the book is Moses's meeting with God atop Mount Sinai. It is there that the fullness of the covenant is proposed, a relationship between the Chosen People and their God freely entered into in love and mutual respect. Once the people ratify God's proposal, this covenant with all its requirements becomes known as the *law*, which would govern Israel religiously, socially, and often politically, for more than a thousand years.

Leviticus: The law. The third volume of the Pentateuch, Leviticus, examines the law in some detail—more detail, as a rule, than most readers are up to. As a result, Leviticus is rarely first choice for bedtime reading, but it does provide particulars necessary for a real understanding of this long-standing relationship between the people of God and their Lord.

Numbers: Counting heads. The book of Numbers takes its name from two censuses, one in chapter 1 and a second in chapter 26. This book carries on the story of the Israelites' sojourn in the Sinai Desert and can be considered an extension of the tale begun in Exodus.

Deuteronomy: The second law. Wherever you run into the prefix *deutero* in the Bible, it means second, so here, in the last book of the Pentateuch, we find a rehash of a lot of material already covered, but it's done in a much different manner. The law is gone over once more, this time in a series of discourses given by Moses as he appeals to the people to live up to the Covenant. As the book ends, the Promised Land—Canaan—is in view, Moses's successor—Joshua—has been appointed, Moses delivers a farewell address (chapters 32—33) and exits the biblical stage.

Historical Books

Joshua: Journey's end. Some say that with the book of Joshua we enter the realm of the Bible's historical books; others say that doesn't happen until we reach the first book of Samuel. Wherever he lands, Joshua is a historical figure and a prominent one. To him fall two heavy responsibilities: (1) To get the Israelites into the Promised Land and conquer such obstacles as lay in his path; and (2) To divide the newly occupied land among the tribes. God selected a very different leader from Moses for these vital tasks. Joshua was a military man, exactly for what the times and situation called.

Judges: But no courts. When we think of judges, the image is usually that of black-robed figures, gavels in hand, presiding over courtrooms. These judges are the furthest thing from magistrates. They are charismatic leaders, often of a military nature, whose assignment is to get the Israelites out of one jam or another. Following the death of Joshua, there is no central authority over the tribes, no leader or governing body.

What remains is a loosely knit confederation of weak tribal units constantly preyed upon by their stronger neighbors. This cycle of being raided and invaded is God's way of getting their attention after major breaches of the covenant which more often than not had something to do with the worship of false gods. Thus sin came and punishment followed. Having their backs to the wall frequently led to fervent repentance and prayers for relief. Help, according to this book, arrived in the form of a judge who took matters (and the offending tribe as well) in hand and whipped everything into shape. Among the more prominent were Deborah, Samson, and Samuel.

Ruth: An interlude. In symphonic concerts, after the orchestra has been working its way through some pretty ponderous pieces, the program may call for an interlude, a light and airy bit to give both musicians and audience a break. The four-chapter gem called the book of Ruth is our interlude. It has almost a fairy-tale quality beginning "Once in the time of the judges..." (Ruth 1:1). Contrary to what was said earlier, this is bedtime reading, short and sweet, with a genuine heroine and better-than-average hero.

Samuel One and Two. The two books of Samuel were, in all probability, originally a single work and may be seen as transition books, wrapping up the period of the judges and introducing the monarchy. Samuel himself plays a dual role: last of the judges and a prophet as well. Hearing the people voice their desire for a king, Samuel reminds them that they already have a king, God, and that they live in a covenanted relationship with that monarch under the law.

What the Israelite leaders really want is someone to fend off the pesky neighbors who have been disturbing the peace throughout the two centuries of the judges. Samuel warns them they'll live to regret their request, but he nonetheless anoints Saul as Israel's first king, a reign that starts well, but ends badly, resulting in Samuel plodding off to Bethlehem to anoint the youngest of Jesse's sons as Saul's successor. And so the greatest of Israel's kings mounts the throne—David, who will be revered through Jewish history as the king of the golden age. The remainder of the books of Samuel recount David's colorful career.

Kings: One and Two. History continues as the books open with David's farewell address and death and continue with the anointing of one of his many sons, Solomon, as the next king.

Most of us have heard of Solomon's wisdom and wealth. Solomon raises Israel to its period of greatest prominence in the Mediterranean world. He builds and builds and builds, but at great cost to his subjects, who pay for it through staggering taxes and conscripted labor. So, upon Solomon's death, a delegation approaches his son, the new king, Rehoboam, begging relief.

Rehoboam, upon consultation with his advisors, takes what is probably is the worst advice given in the entire Bible, telling the people that, if they think they had it tough under his father, they haven't seen anything yet. Whereupon, ten tribes do a little consulting of their own and decide, "Who needs this?" They straightaway secede and establish a kingdom of their own in the north. Hereafter, there will remain two nations: Israel in the north and Judah in the south.

14

The remainder of the books of Kings documents the times of the two nations and their ultimate downfall. Israel is conquered by superpower Assyria in 721 B.C., and most of its citizenry is relocated to other parts of the vast Assyrian Empire, never to return as tribal units, thus becoming known as the *ten lost tribes*. Judah lasts about a century and a half longer, only to fall into the hands of a later superpower, Babylonia, and most Judeans are marched into exile for some eighty years, ending the monarchy.

Chronicles: One more time. The books of Chronicles essentially recap most of what you just read in Kings. They originate from a source which also gives us the next two books, Ezra and Nehemiah. The chronicler condenses the tale, adds a little more theology, and includes the end of the Exile narrative.

Ezra and Nehemiah. Thus, Chronicles sets us up for the post-exilic period of Jewish history and points us right at Ezra and Nehemiah, where we learn about the return of the Judean exiles from Babylon and the rebuilding of their homeland. By this time, all tribal identities except that of Judah have been blurred or lost, and the descendants of Israel have come to be known by the name of that one tribe, Jews.

Tobit, Judith, and Esther: A novel approach. At this point, we get another interlude, a little light reading and a break from all this heavy history. This interlude comes in the form of three relatively short historical novels: Tobit, Judith, and Esther. Each is intriguing in its own way and good for bedtime reading, but if you're all caught up in the historical events, you can skip right past them temporarily and move directly to the final volumes in this section.

First and Second Maccabees: The hammer strikes. Be prepared for another time warp. In First and Second Maccabees, the biblical writers have let something like three centuries slip away without comment and now direct our attention to a time not long before Jesus, the second century B.C. In these books, the Jews are confronted with an attempt to undermine or eliminate their culture, replacing it with the Greek (Hellenistic) traditions so popular in the Mediterranean world of that time. Even the beloved Temple is desecrated.

These books report the attempts of Judas Maccabaeus (the name means *hammer*) and his brothers to regain religious and political freedom. Their success culminates in the glorious rededication of the Temple in a Feast of Light, celebrated today as Hanukkah.

Wisdom Books

The Wisdom Books or the Writings come from a type of literature common in the Near Eastern world in the centuries just before and after Jesus's time. In them, Wisdom is often capitalized and personified and thereafter spoken of as a living being. Some of these books really are wisdom literature: Job, Proverbs, Ecclesiastes, Sirach, and, of course, the book of Wisdom (probably the final contribution to the Old Testament canon, written about 100 B.C. in Alexandria, Egypt).

Each approaches the topic from a different angle. Job ponders the mystery of why the good suffer. Proverbs compiles short axioms as norms for moral conduct (in effect, the Bible's *Poor Richard's Almanac*). In Ecclesiastes, Qoheleth mourns the vanity of everything that is not God, concluding that only God lasts; everything else is transient. Sirach scoops up the wisdom of past centuries and encapsulates it. The book of Wisdom is lyrical in its hope for immortality, the most forceful statement on belief in an afterlife found anywhere in the Old Testament (Wisdom 3—5).

The Song of Songs and the Psalms are strictly speaking not Wisdom literature. The first is an epic love poem, celebrating ideal love between woman and man, which is also seen as an allegory describing the love between God and the Israelites.

With the book of Psalms, we come to the poetry section of the library. We are also face-to-face with liturgical writing, for many of the psalms were Israel's hymns composed over some five hundred years. Sung in Temple, they expressed sentiments ranging from praise and thanksgiving to lamentation, sorrow, and remorse. It has been said that if all the Old Testament were lost to us and only the psalms remained, we would still have nearly all the essential history and theology of those twenty centuries. For instance, in Psalm 137, the exiled Israelites cry, "By the streams of Babylon / we sat and wept / when we remembered

Zion. / On the aspens of that land / we hung up our harps. / ... / How could we sing a song of the Lord / in a foreign land?" Bitterness! Hopelessness! Ah, but there is hope.

The golden thread, though hidden now, is unbroken. God remains faithful to his part of the covenant and holds out a glimmer of hope to his devastated people. For that, we now move to the section of the library known as the Prophets.

Prophetic Books

Most modern Bibles group the prophetic books at the end of the Hebrew Scriptures. They are divided into the *major prophets* and *minor prophets*. The major prophets—Isaiah, Jeremiah, Ezekiel, Daniel—are listed first; major not because their messages are more important, but simply because they are lengthier. From Hosea through Malachi, twelve minor prophets' writings, shorter in length, follow one-by-one.

The main role of the prophets was not to predict the future but to "speak for God" on the issues of the day. They were people called by God, usually to recall the Israelites to their covenant agreement. Frequently, that involved reminders that if the current state of affairs were to continue, the end result would be unpleasant. Hence prophets should be seen against a backdrop of the times and places in which they lived and worked. It is important, for instance, to read Jeremiah in relation to the events preceding the Exile as described in 2 Kings 25 and 2 Chronicles 36.

Every prophet was a product of his time. His primary message to God's people dealt with the current situation and that alone, so when interpreting the prophetic books for our benefit, we should first learn what the initial intent of that message was: What problems of his time was a particular prophet addressing?

Jeremiah, the great prophet in the years immediately prior to the Exile, had warned repeatedly what failure to return to God and his covenant would mean. Like many before and after him, Jeremiah was met with derision and disregard. The call to be a prophet was usually a summons to trial and affliction.

But when the awful consequences did come crashing down on God's people, prophets could also be the bearers of hopeful tidings. During the Exile, with the mighty family tree of David toppled, Jeremiah says, "Behold, the days are coming, says the Lord, when I will raise up a righteous shoot to David. As king he shall reign and govern wisely. He shall do what is just and right in the land" (Jeremiah 23:5–6).

The man who holds out the strongest "thread" of hope to the exiled Israelites is Ezekiel, who became a prophet in Babylon. Although the opening chapters of the book of Ezekiel are largely rebukes to Israel for its many transgressions, the latter section is filled with the bright vision of salvation in a new covenant. He speaks soothingly of a wonderful return to the land of promise.

How will this happen? Who will this be? The concept remains dim and ill-defined for now. But when Israel returns from its captivity and begins to rebuild, there will be ever increasing speculation on this "righteous shoot to David" (23:5).

In time, this person takes on a more focused description. To succeed to David's throne, he would have to be a king, probably a strong and good king like David himself. He would be of David's tribe, Judah, and David's hometown, Bethlehem, and he would be commissioned for his task in the manner of Israelite priests, prophets, and kings; he would be anointed with holy oil. The Hebrew word for an anointed one was *Messiah*. In the prevailing Greek of Jesus's day, the term would be *Christos*.

Questions for Reflection

1. What is a covenant and what is our covenant relationship with God?
2. What do you think forms parts of your covenant with God?
3. Describe the thread that links together all of the forty-six books of the Old Testament.

CHAPTER THREE

The New Testament

We now enter that section of the library called the New Testament (covenant) or the Christian Scriptures, and still the golden thread moves on, surfacing next at the beginning of the Gospel of Matthew, where we are faced with one of those lengthy genealogies of which Scripture is so fond, one has much to say to us. Matthew, who was unique in that he was writing for a Christian community composed largely of converts from Judaism, launches into his account of Jesus with this first verse of his first chapter: "A family record of Jesus Christ, son of David, son of Abraham."

In one opening shot, Matthew has presented Jesus as the Christ (*Christos*), the Messiah. He has also positioned him firmly in the line of those towering figures to whom the covenant promises were made: Abraham, David, but no Moses? Matthew is saving that only for a moment. It quickly becomes clear that he wants his audience to see Jesus as the new Moses. Thus, Matthew and Matthew alone tells the story of Jesus being saved while infants all around him are being slaughtered just as Moses was saved while Hebrew boys who were his contemporaries died. Only Matthew informs us of the Holy Family's trek to Egypt. Jesus will come forth from there in the same manner Moses did. In Matthew, exclusively, Jesus's most famous sermon is situated on a hillside or mount from which he will deepen and broaden the requirements of the covenant just as Moses did on Sinai, only this time it will be done on Jesus's own authority, thereby equating him with God.

Matthew's version of Jesus's ancestry is stylized: "from Abraham to David, fourteen generations; from David to the Babylonian captivity, fourteen generations; from the Babylonian captivity to the Messiah, fourteen generations" (Matthew 1:17). And Jesus is born in David's city, Bethlehem, a fact which Matthew mentions five times for emphasis. There's no doubt about it, according to Matthew: Jesus is the anointed one, the Christ, the Messiah, the son of David, the one who will fulfill the promise made to that great king. And throughout his Gospel, Matthew maintains the kingdom as a major theme, showing through a multitude of references to the Hebrew Scriptures that David's line will continue forever. Jesus will be King of Kings in an eternal kingdom where all those covenanted to him and his father will dwell forever. The promise is fulfilled. That's the Gospel truth.

Although Matthew's Gospel has received special notice, there are three more such books in this library that is the Bible: Mark, Luke, and John. Reading them all provides us with four distinctive perspectives on Jesus and four distinctive proclamations of the Gospel (good news): the Messiah has come and with him salvation for those who live in covenant with him! The golden thread still gleams as Jesus draws his inner circle around him for the Last Supper. Near the end of the meal, raising his cup of wine, he surveys them lovingly and announces, "This cup is the new covenant in my blood which shall be shed for you" (Luke 22:20).

And still the full length of the golden thread has not spun from the spool. As followers of Jesus fan out around the Mediterranean, great missionaries like Paul work devotedly to keep the fledgling Christian communities faithful to this new covenant, not an easy task in a first-century world singularly lacking in rapid transportation and efficient communication. The result is a flurry of letters, some of which are preserved for us in this biblical library. Paul, John, James, Peter, Jude, and others write to one or another of these young churches to explain, to expound, to upbraid, to uphold, to smooth the way for the golden thread as it winds through new territory which will ultimately take it all over the globe.

Where does the golden thread end? Actually, it has the same end we have ourselves: heaven, where we will live forever covenanted to our God. And the last book in the Bible glows with heavenly light. Here, in veiled and symbolic terminology, are the apocalyptic visions of the book of Revelation. By turns haunting and bewildering, these visions come to rest at last at the throne of God.

The Four Gospels
How Were They Written?

Since the Gospels were written for Christians, we must start with the central event of Christian history and Christian faith: *the resurrection of Jesus.* If ever the expression, "It blew their minds," is proper, it is apt to describe what happened to the followers of Jesus as they experienced the risen Jesus and then began to realize who that mysterious, attractive man really was—is.

At the same time, other followers of Jesus would also gather to remember and retell. The sick would remember some days more fondly, sinners others. Those who would have to debate publicly would remember what suited their need. If you were hungry, you would remember bread. If you were being ground into poverty, you would remember the Beatitudes, the story of the rich man and Lazarus.

The Church in Jerusalem might emphasize the cleansing of the Temple and not recall Jesus's going to the Gentiles. In Galilee, the

Church might stress the stories that centered around the lake and merely summarize Jesus's baptism down in Judea.

The stories of Jesus would be told at the gatherings for Eucharist. Gradually there would be collections of stories, told and retold over the years. Scholars have found that folk memory preserves detached units best; for instance, general sayings of Jesus apart from any particular situation; or stories that lead up to a punch line (e.g., "Give to Caesar what is Caesar's, but give to God what is God's"—Mark 12:13–17); or narratives with almost no words of Jesus, but colorful details centering on a miracle (e.g., the storm on the lake—Mark 4:35–41). The units were told in patterns that made them easy to remember. As time went on, these separate units would be polished to smoothness like stones in the daily tide.

When the first Christian preachers went forth, it was not with tape recorders and movie projectors. They proclaimed *the meaning of Jesus* in terms the people could understand, in the Jewish way to Jews, in the Greek way to Greeks.

The only "bible" they had was what we call the Old Testament, the Hebrew Scriptures. They found Jesus in its pages. He was the fulfillment of all that had been promised. His life, death, and Resurrection were "according to the Scriptures." But they were gradually (many without realizing it) building up what we call the New Testament, at first in oral and then in written collections.

By saying the final result was inspired, we mean that the Holy Spirit guarantees the truthfulness and trustworthiness of what human beings said and wrote in human ways.

What Are the Different Approaches?

We can discern several reasons for the rich variety of approaches in the four Gospels.

First, each writer selected some stories and sayings rather than others, according to his individual purpose and viewpoint. The "seven last words" of Jesus are not all together in any one Gospel: Luke has three of them, Matthew and Mark share one, John has the other three. Matthew has eight beatitudes; Luke has only four, but he parallels them with four woes. John has no account of the institution of the Eucharist. The baptism of Jesus is progressively deemphasized in the four Gospels. The "Our Father" is slightly different in Luke and Matthew. All this is the result of the authors' varying emphases and intentions.

Second, the Gospel writers, speaking for and in the Church, and following the practice of the Church, shaped the words of Jesus, adapted them to apply to new situations, ones that did not exist when Jesus spoke. We have seen that the apostles themselves did this. Jesus would not have said, to Jews, for instance, that a woman could not divorce her husband (Mark 10:12). This was unheard of in Jewish law. But among Greeks it was possible, so Jesus's full meaning had to be expressed.

Matthew and Mark describe Jesus as dying with a loud cry, but they do not record any words; in Luke, Jesus says, "Father, into your hands I commend my spirit" (23:46). Some scholars feel that Luke's expression of trust is parallel to "My God, my God, why have you forsaken me?" in Matthew (27:46). In John, Jesus says, "Now it is finished" (19:30). They are three artists painting the same sunset.

The Gospel writers often had to vary their accounts because the communities for which they wrote were so different.

Some were widely scattered, some in totally pagan areas, some close to the Jerusalem tradition, some being persecuted, some living in peace. For converts, certain questions had to be asked. For Greeks, certain Jewish customs had to be explained.

To sum up, then: While there is a vast amount of similarity in the Gospels (especially the first three), the individual writers did have their own purposes, and employed techniques of selection, adaptation, and modification. It should be evident that the Gospels are not mere "lives of Jesus." They are the Church's attempt to proclaim to various people in various situations the meaning of Jesus. The Gospels should not be seen as photographed, tape-recorded biographies.

The Gospel Writers

According to Father Donald Senior, C.P., in *Jesus: A Gospel Portrait,* an overemphasis on the Gospels as sources of biographical information about Jesus could distort our understanding of what they are and thus blunt their power. As is often repeated today by New Testament scholars, the Gospels are not "biographies" in the technical sense.

If the Gospels are not technically a biography, then what are they?

Too often the working image we have of the evangelists is they were mere secretaries for divine dictation, and the Gospels as books practically dropped from heaven. In fact, the process by which the Gospels came into existence was much more complex—and much richer. The more we know about the real process, the more we can understand how to read a Gospel and how to savor the portrait of Jesus it provides.

The Gospels: A Record of Faith

What shall we call them, then? Perhaps it would be best to use the phrase "faith-record," testimonies of faith addressed to those who are the faithful. They cannot be used to "prove" anything to pagans or scientists or Hindus.

Remember, it was a loving group (no matter how undependable and obtuse of mind) that listened to Jesus. The Gospels are not the Pharisees' notion of Jesus, but the picture that developed in the minds of those who loved him, the community we call Church.

We must remember that it was the Church who wrote the New Testament (just as it was the Jewish people who wrote the "Old")—this loving group of followers. They painted the masterpiece gradually, a touch here, a touch there, as an artist gradually puts his subject on canvas. Individual authors (probably a succession) put their stamp on the finished product, but the Word of God was heard and written within the faith of the community.

It is therefore important to remember that the Gospel writers did not go off to their ivory towers to write. Though they each had their own purposes, they were expressing the basic faith record that had been developed in the meditation and prayer of the Church and by the light of the Holy Spirit.

The Church rejected whatever accounts did not have an authentic ring to them—there are several noncanonical Gospels filled with marvelous accounts of supposed incidents in Jesus's life. But these were not incorporated into the New Testament.

The Different Gospel Narratives

Mark's Narrative(s). Most scholars recognize that Mark's original narrative consisted of 16:1–8. Because of the brief, almost unfinished character of that account, however, early Christians added other endings. The best known of these is 16:9–20. Thus we may speak of two "Marcan" accounts of the Resurrection.

Mark 16:1–8, which is basically the story of the empty tomb, contains the heavenly revelation that Jesus is risen and promises his appearance in Galilee to the other disciples and Peter. Yet that appearance is never described, and the story ends with the women leaving the tomb afraid and silent.

Only through suffering will the disciples reach fuller understanding. Throughout the Gospel, Mark emphasizes how difficult it was for those who followed Jesus to believe in him fully because they did not understand that suffering and rejection were an essential part of the identity of God's Son. In the great trial of Jesus's passion the male disciples have all failed and run away—an experience reflecting fear and shameful weakness. But their pain leads to light. After they have suffered and failed Jesus will appear to them in Galilee (Mark 14:27–28).

Faith comes from a personal understanding of the risen Lord. Of course, Mark does not mean that Jesus's followers were permanently silent and afraid. The added ending (Mark 16:9–20) recognizes that point by showing how an encounter with the risen Jesus brought about faith.

Matthew's Narrative. As always, Matthew, although he draws on Mark, is the more skilled teacher, kinder to readers who do not always see implications. Mark 16:1–8 does not actually describe appearances of the risen Jesus, but Matthew does. Thus in 28:9, Matthew tells of an appearance to the women after they left the tomb—an appearance (echoed in John and Mark 16:9) that may well represent ancient tradition even though it was never part of the official preaching (such as reported by Paul in 1 Corinthians 15).

An attempt to block the Resurrection of Jesus. Even more dramatically, in Matthew 27:62–66, 28:4, 11–15, we are told of a scheme to frustrate the Resurrection by getting Pilate's soldiers to guard Jesus's tomb. One of the tragic elements in Matthew's Christian experience is a hostile relationship between synagogue authorities and Christian believers. That is reflected from start to finish in Matthew's Gospel.

At the very beginning of his Gospel, Matthew portrayed King Herod, the chief priests, and the scribes plotting to destroy the newly born Messiah (2:3–5, 16–18, 20); but God frustrated them. So now at the end of the Gospel, Matthew portrays the prefect Pilate, the chief priests, and the Pharisees plotting against Jesus. Once more God intervenes to frustrate them. Matthew reminds us that the Christian proclamation of the Gospel will not be without struggle.

Jesus in Galilee promises to be "with us" always. Last of all Matthew describes what Mark only promised: the appearance of Jesus to the disciples in Galilee. In Matthew's opening of the public ministry in Galilee (chapters 5 through 7) Jesus delivered on a mountain a "sermon" that contained the essentials of his new teaching about the Kingdom of God. In 10:6–7, Jesus sent his disciples to preach that kingdom "to the lost sheep of the house of Israel." Now from Galilee the risen Jesus sends his disciples forth to teach "all nations," making them disciples by baptizing them.

Matthew is careful to show that God's plan for Jesus was consistent from beginning to end. The revelation given about Jesus before he was born proclaimed that he would be Emmanuel ("God with us"—1:23); Jesus's last words are "I am with you all days to the end of time" (28:20).

Luke's Narrative. Like Matthew, Luke follows Mark in the basic story of the empty tomb, but then goes his own way in the appearances he reports. While Matthew recounts an appearance of Jesus in Jerusalem to two women, Luke recounts at length (24:13–35) the appearance of Jesus to two male disciples on the road from Jerusalem to Emmaus. In the Acts of the Apostles (2:42,46; 20:7,11), which Luke also authored as a sequel to his Gospel account, he will point to the role of "the breaking of the bread" in Christian community life. He prepares for that in the Emmaus story by having the disciples recognize Jesus in the breaking of the bread.

Luke sees the Resurrection as fulfilling the Scriptures. Then Luke turns to the appearance of the risen Jesus to the Eleven (the twelve disciples minus Judas). More than either Mark or Matthew, Luke stresses what was already implicit in the empty tomb: the reality of the body of the risen Jesus who was not simply a spirit (24:37–43). Particularly significant is that the risen Jesus teaches the Eleven about his death and Resurrection by explaining the Scriptures, "All the things written about me in the Law of Moses, and in the Prophets, and in the Psalms must be fulfilled" (24:44).

Luke's emphasis is preparing the way for the Church life he will describe in his Acts of the Apostles, where Peter, Stephen, and Paul begin their preaching by emphasizing that the Scriptures anticipate what happened to Jesus (Acts 2:14–21; 7:1–50; 13:16–22).

Luke spotlights Jerusalem as the setting for Jesus's appearances and ascension. Matthew has the appearance of the risen Jesus to the Eleven take place in Galilee. This region was a fitting selection from the tradition for Matthew's purpose since for him Galilee is the land of the Gentiles (4:15) and Jesus after his Resurrection is instructing his disciples to go and make disciples of the Gentiles (28:19). Luke has the appearance to the Eleven take place in Jerusalem. This was a fitting selection from the tradition for his purpose. For him, the Gospel began with the appearance of Gabriel to Zechariah in the Jerusalem Temple; now it ends with Jesus's disciples in the Temple blessing God.

Most of us are familiar with the imagery at the beginning of Acts (1:3, 9–12) where Jesus ascends into heaven from the Mount of Olives forty days after the Resurrection. Yet at the very end of the Gospel (24:50–51), Luke has him ascend into heaven from the same region on Easter Sunday night.

In this "double exposure" we see Luke's theological perceptivity. In one sense (dramatically portrayed in the Gospel) Jesus's return to God was the end of his earthly career, a career beginning and ending in Jerusalem and thus symbolically lived within the confines of Judaism. In another sense (dramatically portrayed in Acts) Jesus's return to God begins the life of the Church that starts in Jerusalem (Judaism) and extends to Rome (the Gentile world).

John's Narrative. The account in chapter 20 of John, like Luke and Mark 16:9–20, has the appearances of Jesus take place in Jerusalem. The account in chapter 21 (which is only superficially connected to chapter 20), like Matthew and Mark 16:7, has the appearance of Jesus take place in Galilee. Each chapter is appropriate to John's thought, but in a different way.

John's Gospel narrates a series of encounters as character after character comes to meet Jesus in center stage and react to him. This atmosphere continues in chapter 20 where sequentially Peter and the Beloved Disciple, Mary Magdalene, the disciples, and Thomas encounter the mystery of Jesus's resurrection.

The Beloved Disciple is the first to believe. In the tradition (1 Corinthians 15:5; Luke 24:34), Simon Peter was the first among the male disciples of Jesus to see the risen Jesus. John does not violate that but still exemplifies his peculiar emphasis:

Throughout the latter part of the Gospel the unnamed Beloved Disciple, the one particularly loved by Jesus, is closer than Peter to the master. In 20:3–10 where Peter and the Beloved Disciple go to the tomb, neither sees Jesus; but the Beloved Disciple comes to faith without an appearance of the Risen One.

Mary Magdalene is the first to proclaim the risen Lord. As in Matthew and the added ending of Mark, Mary Magdalene is the first follower to see the risen Jesus. She does not recognize him by sight but does when he calls her name, fulfilling the prediction of the Good Shepherd in 10:3–5 that he would call by name the sheep that belong to him, and they would follow him. Jesus speaks to her of "my Father and your Father" and refers to his disciples as his "brothers." Thus to Magdalene, Jesus fulfills the promise in John's Prologue (1:12): "All those who did accept him he empowered to become God's children." With this revelation Mary goes forth to announce, "I have seen the Lord." If the Beloved Disciple was the first to believe, Mary becomes the first to proclaim the Risen Lord.

Jesus's disciples are "re-created" by the Holy Spirit. Next (John 20:19–23) Jesus appears to the group of disciples, consisting of or including members of the Twelve. Just as in Genesis 2:7 the Lord God formed a human being out of the dust of the earth by breathing into his nostrils the breath of life, so Jesus breathes on the disciples and they receive the Holy Spirit, recreating them as God's children with eternal life. For them this is the birth of the

Spirit promised in John 3:5. Throughout the Gospel, Jesus has referred to himself as the one sent by God; the disciples are now sent to continue his work in the world with his power over evil and sin.

Thomas the doubter. The various Gospels mention doubt when Jesus appears to his followers after the Resurrection (Matthew 28:17; Luke 24:37–38; Mark 16:14), but in 20:24–29 John dramatizes that doubt in an individual. Paradoxically, however, from the lips of this "doubting Thomas" comes the highest confession of faith in all the Gospels: "My Lord and my God." The Gospel began with the Prologue's affirmation (1:1), "The Word was God." Now human beings have come to recognize that.

Peter as missionary and pastor. Chapter 21 moves the setting to Galilee and highlights two scenes related to Simon Peter's career. A miraculous catch of fish directed by the risen Jesus is dragged ashore by Peter, a symbol of the missionary role he will have. But then abruptly the symbolism shifts as Peter is commissioned to feed Jesus's sheep. The shift reflects Christian experience: A great missionary thrust in the first generations eventually ceded to pastoral care for those brought to Christ.

Stories Told It Best

Our Christian ancestors spoke about the Resurrection long before they wrote about it. The first believers proclaimed the truth by word of mouth in forceful slogans and exclamations: "The Lord was raised indeed, and has appeared to Simon [Peter]" (Luke 24:34). In Jerusalem in particular, biting challenges are recalled associating the Crucifixion and the Resurrection: "You crucified this Jesus...but God raised him up" (Acts 2:23–24; 4:10; 5:30–31; 10:39–40).

Four steps are mentioned by Paul in a formula delivered to him from the earliest days of his coming to faith: "That Christ died... that he was buried, that he was raised on the third day according to the Scriptures, and that he appeared" (1 Corinthians 15:3–5). What this sequence of events means for Jews and Gentiles alike is explained by Paul: Jesus was "put to death for our trespasses and raised for our justification" (Romans 4:25).

As vivid as these proclamations were, the story form proved to be a more effective way of conveying the full impact of the Resurrection. The association between the Crucifixion and the Resurrection needed to be fleshed out in a dramatic way so that those who were not present in Jerusalem could understand what God had done in making Jesus victorious over death. Consequently, the Gospel stories are quite different from the brief formulas preserved for us from the early preaching.

These brief, spoken formulas never mentioned the finding of Jesus's empty tomb. Yet in all four Gospels the empty tomb becomes the important link between the Crucifixion and the Resurrection—spotlighted as the site of the revelation that Jesus has conquered death. His followers saw his body placed in the tomb before the Sabbath began; but when the Sabbath was over, his body was no longer there. What happened?

The appearances of the risen Jesus led Christians to a faith that enabled them to look back and see that the empty tomb itself already could be understood as a revelation that Jesus was no longer dead.

In all four Gospels an angel or angels appear at the tomb to make the meaning of the empty tomb crystal clear. The Gospels vary in their descriptions of the angel(s), whether there are one or two, and whether they are outside or inside the tomb, sitting or standing. These are the variations to be expected in a story transmitted orally. But the basic message of the angels is the same: Jesus is no longer in the tomb because he has been raised!

The way in which the appearances are described tells us that the Resurrection was no mere resuscitation of Jesus to ordinary life. When the risen Jesus appeared, he was not easily recognizable even to those who knew him well (for example, Mary Magdalene and Simon Peter). He could pass through locked doors; cover distances instantaneously; and yet he still pointed to his body as real. Thus there is no evidence whatsoever that early preaching ever involved anything other than a bodily resurrection that involved tremendous transformation.

Acts of the Apostles

The book of Acts is the only New Testament document devoted exclusively to the story of the early Church. It is the companion volume to the Gospel of Luke (compare the Prologues, Luke 1:1–4, and Acts 1:1–5).

In order to provide the proper framework for reflecting on Acts, we should note first its general outline. The book has four main sections: Prologue (1:1–5); The Mission of the Church in Jerusalem and Environs (1:6—8:3); The Mission of the Church in Judea and Samaria (8:4—12:25); and The Mission of the Church to the Ends of the Earth (13:1—28:31).

Acts gives a clue to this outline at 1:8. There the Risen Jesus promises the gift of the Holy Spirit who will enable the apostles to be emboldened and to embark on worldwide missionary activity. The text reads: "But you will receive power when the Holy Spirit has come upon you; and you will be my witnesses in Jerusalem, in all Judea and Samaria, and to the ends of the earth."

If Acts presents the essential character of the Church as an evangelizing community, it has much more to say about the qualities of Church life.

Everyone, Everywhere. First, Acts reveals a Church which is a multicultural, universal community. One should not miss the fact that Easter Sunday the first reading taken from Acts is an excerpt of Peter's speech at the conversion of Cornelius and his household, who were Gentiles from Caesarea (10:34–42).

Peter begins by noting that "I truly understand that God shows no partiality, but in every nation anyone who fears him and does what is right is acceptable to him" (10:34–35).

Peter confirms this judgment at the Council of Jerusalem, at which the Church more formally permitted the mission to the Gentiles (Acts 15). Between Easter and Pentecost, the liturgical year recounts the conversion stories of many others of differing ethnic and cultural backgrounds. They all provide testimony to the effectiveness of God's power, at work through the apostolic preaching, in bringing people to Christ.

This theme of the universal appeal of Christ returns at the end of the Easter season, like a matching bookend.

Pentecost is the quintessential story of universalism. The Holy Spirit descends on the apostles and enables them to speak in tongues mirroring the nations of the known world (2:1–11).

A great hallmark of the Catholic Church has always been its openness to this diversity. *Catholic* (from the Greek *katholikos*) means "universal." Peter points out how Jesus Christ fulfills God's promise to Abraham that in him "all the families of the earth shall be blessed" (3:25). Languages and accents may differ, customs and styles of dress may vary, but the Easter season testifies to the universal call of Jesus Christ.

Witness and Suffering. A prominent feature of Acts is the regular presentation of stories about giving witness in word and deed to the message of Jesus Christ, even in the midst of suffering. The Greek word for *witness* is the same as the English word *martyr*. Many of the stories of Acts heard throughout the Easter season remind us of the price our ancestors in faith paid for proclaiming the Gospel message.

While Stephen's martyrdom is the prime model of witness for Acts (7:54—8:1), not all the persecutions end in death. Peter, John, Paul, and others throughout Acts suffer imprisonment, beatings, trials, and numerous other tribulations for the sake of testifying to their faith in Jesus Christ as the crucified and risen Savior of the world. At times, God sends them miraculous aid (for example, when Paul and Silas were imprisoned in Philippi, 16:22–34).

At other times, the resourcefulness of the apostles themselves leads to a respite in their persecution (see Paul before the Sanhedrin, 23:6–11). In either case, the goal is said to be the same. The Church must give testimony in good times and in bad, in suffering and in success. In all cases, the community is to "bear witness" to Jesus (23:11).

Christian Essentials. Third, the Church of Acts is a community of prayer, worship, and joy. "They devoted themselves to the apostles' teaching and fellowship, to the breaking of bread and the prayers" (2:42).

The reading goes on to describe how all the members of the community shared their property in common. "Fellowship" included sharing goods with other members of the community (4:32–35).

They broke bread in their homes (2:46), a New Testament expression for celebrating the Eucharist. Acts thus highlights the sacramental dimension of the community.

Acts also recalls the pervading attitude of joy and exultation, a joy rooted in the resurrection of Jesus. That joy resounds in the life of the Church, even in times of persecution (2:47; 5:41; 13:52; 15:3).

Such idealistic descriptions are reminders of the true nature of the Church community. But we might ask a legitimate question: How realistic is this picture? Acts hints at times that all was not perfect. One is the curious story of Ananias and Sapphira (5:1–11). This married couple withheld from the common pot proceeds from the sale of some property. Peter confronts them and denounces their selfishness. Their punishment seems rather severe, for, upon Peter's interrogation about their evil deception, they both drop dead!

Work of the Spirit. Lastly, the Church described in Acts expects to succeed because the Holy Spirit is behind, within, and underneath it all. From beginning to end, the book of Acts shows the power of the Holy Spirit at work in the life of the Church.

Luke emphasizes that everything that took place in the earthly life of Jesus and then that of the early Church was all part of God's mysterious plan of salvation, guided by the Holy Spirit. Luke emphasizes this, for example, by speaking of the "necessity" of the suffering, death, and Resurrection of Jesus as the Messiah (Luke 24:7, 44–46; Acts 1:16).

This divine necessity, because it is accomplished under the guidance of the Holy Spirit, applies to the apostles as well. Thus

Paul is told of the necessity of his bearing witness in Rome (19:21; 23:11).

For Acts, the Holy Spirit is the "promise of the Father" (Acts 1:4; see Luke 24:49). The Spirit comes to the apostles only after the ascension of Jesus takes place, forty days after the Resurrection (Acts 1:6–12). The forty days, a symbolic biblical period of instruction and preparation to accomplish God's will, allows for the apostles to be prepared for their subsequent mission. They are then ready to receive the Holy Spirit and to be emboldened with courage. Although the Spirit is often behind the scenes, Acts makes it quite clear that the spread of the Gospel—the success of the apostolic preaching—is due entirely to the Spirit's guidance.

St. Paul the Apostle

St. Paul is the most prominent personality of the New Testament, apart from Jesus himself. Thirteen of the twenty seven books of the New Testament bear his name. All of them are letters. Much of what we know about Paul comes from these remarkable written sources, supplemented by stories from the Acts of the Apostles, in which Paul figures prominently in the second half (Acts 9—28).

Paul, also known by his Jewish name, Saul (Acts 13:9), was born in Tarsus, Cilicia, in Asia Minor (now modern-day Turkey) probably between 1 and 10 A.D. He was a diaspora Jew, that is, a

Jew living outside the homeland of Palestine. Tarsus was a large, prosperous city in the Roman Empire, so it is quite fair to call Paul an urbanite. He was likely well-educated, apparently a student of the great rabbi Gamaliel I in Jerusalem (Acts 22:3).

Paul's call and mission. Paul himself admits that he persecuted the Church out of zeal for his Jewish background. However, around the year 35 A.D. he had a remarkable experience. On the road to Damascus, the risen Lord, Jesus, appeared to him and called him to be "the apostle to the Gentiles" (Acts 9:1–19). Paul never describes this event in detail. Rather, he speaks of a "revelation of Jesus Christ" (Galatians 1:12) that leaves the impression of a supernatural appearance of the resurrected Jesus, or perhaps what we might call a mystical experience.

Like Jesus, Paul was born a Jew and lived his entire life as a Jew. He was quite proud of his Jewish heritage. In Philippians, he summarizes his background thus: "circumcised on the eighth day, a member of the people of Israel, of the tribe of Benjamin, a Hebrew born of Hebrews; as to the law, a Pharisee; as to zeal, a persecutor of the church; as to righteousness under the law, blameless" (Philippians 3:5–6).

Paul would not characterize his experience as a "conversion" in the sense of a change of religion—he never claims to have abandoned Judaism—but more likely as a "call" or "commission." Acts portrays the event in terms reminiscent of the call of Old Testament prophets, and this is consistent with Paul's own

44

description found in Acts. Paul considers himself an "apostle," one who has been called and sent by the Lord Jesus himself for a special mission. He was to bring the Gentiles into the fold of those who accepted Jesus of Nazareth as the long-awaited Messiah, the savior of the world.

Paul's mission as evangelizer. After his call, Paul began an intense ministry of evangelization. He took up (or returned to) the work of tent making so that he would not be a burden to the communities he served. After a mysterious three-year period in Arabia, he went to Jerusalem to meet with Peter, James (the brother of the Lord) and John (in about 38 A.D.). They were leaders of the new movement of Jesus's followers in Jerusalem that Acts calls "the Way" and who eventually became known as "Christians."

These leaders apparently endorsed Paul's mission to the Gentiles. Paul, accompanied by colleagues, then went over the next twelve years to Syria, Cilicia, and Galatia and eventually crossed over into Europe to proclaim the Gospel of Jesus Christ in Macedonia, Achaia, and throughout the Mediterranean region to "the ends of the earth" (Acts 1:8).

Paul's ministry was missionary evangelization, which he exercised with great effect. He established communities of faith in many major cities of the Roman Empire, such as Ephesus, Corinth, Philippi, and Thessalonica.

Teaching through letter writing. In the last decade or more of his life, Paul not only continued his missionary activity but also wrote letters (from about the years 50 to 60). The letters that survive in our New Testament, in their canonical order, are: Romans, 1 and 2 Corinthians, Galatians, Ephesians, Philippians, Colossians, 1 and 2 Thessalonians, 1 and 2 Timothy, Titus, and Philemon. Letters afforded him an excellent means to stay in touch with the communities that he founded on his various missions.

At times, Paul would write from prison, one of the many experiences of suffering he endured as a follower of Jesus. At other times he would write to admonish his communities, to instruct them, to encourage them and to express his plans for the future. The earliest letter of Paul is First Thessalonians (50–51 A.D.); the last letter is either Romans or Philemon (written sometime between 58 and 60 A.D.).

By any estimation, Paul was a formidable personality. He argued persuasively with the well-known early Christian leaders, especially Peter and James, over the need to adapt the Gospel of Jesus Christ to the Gentiles (Galatians 2:11–14). He also had no trouble sternly reprimanding his communities whenever he thought they had strayed from the Gospel he preached.

But he also loved his communities dearly and treated them as good parents treat their children, comparing himself to a nursing mother (1 Thessalonians 2:11) and elsewhere as their "father."

More important, Paul's letters contain tremendous insights into the spiritual life. Paul explicitly desired that his communities become "holy." He tells the Thessalonians outright, "For this is the will of God, your sanctification" (1 Thessalonians 4:3a). He reminds the Ephesians "to clothe yourselves with the new self, created according to the likeness of God in true righteousness and holiness" (Ephesians 4:24). Holiness meant becoming more and more Godlike. He writes that holiness is our destiny as Christians, but is not something people accomplish on their own. True holiness comes about only by surrendering ourselves to God's will and to God's power.

Questions for Reflection

1. How does St. Paul speak to you today?
2. How does Acts of the Apostles show that the Church is missionary and universal?
3. Why did the four Gospel writers vary their accounts and what do they say to us today?

CHAPTER FOUR

How to Read the Bible

Where to Open Your Bible

What is the best way to begin reading this library which is the Bible? One way *not* to do it is by starting at page one and plowing through to the end. That makes about as much sense as starting with the first book on the top shelf of the library and reading every book in order. The Bible was just not meant to be read that way, and most readers who try it lose their enthusiasm before they get through the Old Testament book of Leviticus.

One good place to begin is the Acts of the Apostles. This is the story of the early Church, and especially of the missionary work of St. Paul. It is not difficult to catch the author's excitement about the work of the Spirit in the newborn Christian community. After reading in Acts about the early Christians of Thessalonica and Corinth and Philippi, it becomes much more interesting to read the letters St. Paul wrote to those churches.

These letters will arouse your curiosity about the first books of the Bible, to which Paul often refers, and you will enjoy reading Genesis, Exodus, and Deuteronomy. By then you will be ready to reread the Gospels, noticing the new light that is cast on many passages by your Old Testament reading.

Then you might want to turn to the book of Psalms, which summarizes the history and spirituality of the Old Testament, and contains the prayers actually used by Jesus, Mary, and all the first Christians. By this point, the Bible will have become a world familiar to you. You will have visited its high points and will be ready to explore whichever of the lesser paths may appeal to you.

Some Tips for Reading, Studying, and Praying the Bible

Reading Your Bible

Don't begin at the beginning or end. Begin with the familiar. For Christians the New Testament is a better place to start than the Old Testament. Perhaps begin with Mark, the shortest Gospel, or the letters of Paul. Do *not* start with the book of Revelation, a complex and symbolic book.

Read sections rather than sentences. The Bible will make more sense if you pay attention to sections that are grouped together.

Read aloud. Everyone used to do it, especially when the books of the Bible were written. The Bible was meant to be *heard*—it originated as an oral tradition. Reading aloud involves you more completely than reading silently.

Studying Your Bible

Read the introductions. Most Bibles have introductions added by the editors, and they will prepare you for what comes next. Read the introduction first!

Read the footnotes. The Bible often contains material that is very foreign to our world. Customs, terms, symbolic names are among those concepts that often require explanation. The footnotes are there for everyone, not just for scholars.

Use the cross-references. Most Bibles place these references to other biblical passages in the footnotes or on the side of the page. Often New Testament passages contain quotations or allusions to Old Testament passages. These cross-references will help you further understand what you are studying. This takes some time, but your reward will be a richer understanding of the text.

Be flexible in your interpretations. You don't need to be afraid of misinterpreting the Bible if you remember that your interpretation is not necessarily *the* interpretation. This is especially good in a group setting: Sharing ideas about Bible passages is a wonderful way of studying the Bible, especially when you remain open to further guidance about your views. The ideal group would have a leader with some professional experience, or who has taken time to carefully learn and prepare a historical or scientific perspective.

Praying Your Bible Outside of Mass

Invoke the Holy Spirit. Every time you sit down to pray with the Bible, begin with a brief prayer to call upon the guidance of the Holy Spirit. Something as simple as "Come, Holy Spirit, be my guide as I try to understand this Word" reminds us that we need to surrender to God in order to understand the Scriptures properly.

Choose a passage to reflect on. Working through the whole book of the Bible prayerfully is more effective than random interpretations. Another way of doing this is to pray along with the lectionary selections for the upcoming Sunday Mass. That can help you prepare to hear the Word more fruitfully when it is proclaimed and preached upon the following Sunday. In three years' time, you'll have prayed along with most of the Bible!

Read the passage once through fully. Getting the big picture first helps you understand each section or passage better.

Read each section of the passage slowly. Slow, meditative reading is an ancient Christian practice known as *lectio divina*. Sitting with the text, mulling over its words and phrases, and soaking in its images or themes, truly brings one to a prayerful understanding.

Let the words sink in, and you will feel yourself in the presence of God.

Use your imagination. Although this approach may not work for every passage, it can be very prayerful for some. Imagine yourself in the text. Where are you? Are there characters with whom you identify? Do you see yourself in any actions?

Reread the entire passage. Once you have spent time reflecting on some sections of a passage, reread it in its entirety. Though some parts may have spoken to you more clearly, this exercise will help you remember to keep the section in context.

Conclude with a prayer of thanksgiving. Thank God for the gift of the Word as you conclude your prayer exercise. It is God's Word that gives us life.

Questions for Reflection

1. How has the Bible been an influence for you and for your family?
2. What would you most like to gain from reading the Bible?
3. How would you go about achieving this?

The Books of the Bible

THE OLD TESTAMENT

Pentateuch or Torah
Genesis
Exodus
Leviticus
Numbers
Deuteronomy
Historical Books
Joshua
Judges
Ruth
1 Samuel
2 Samuel
1 Kings
2 Kings
1 Chronicles
2 Chronicles
Ezra

Nehemiah
Tobit
Judith
Esther
1 Maccabees
2 Maccabees
Wisdom Books
Job
Psalms
Proverbs
Ecclesiastes
Song of Songs
Wisdom
Sirach
Prophetic Books
Isaiah
Jeremiah

Lamentations
Baruch
Ezekiel
Daniel
Hosea
Joel
Amos
Obadiah
Jonah
Micah
Nahum
Habakkuk
Zephaniah
Haggai
Zechariah
Malachi

THE NEW TESTAMENT

Gospels
Matthew
Mark
Luke
John
Acts of the Apostles
Letters of St. Paul
Romans
1 Corinthians
2 Corinthians
Galatians

Ephesians
Philippians
Colossians
1 Thessalonians
2 Thessalonians
1 Timothy
2 Timothy
Titus
Philemon
Other Letters
Hebrews

James
1 Peter
2 Peter
1 John
2 John
3 John
Jude
Apocalypse
Revelation

Sources

Brown, Raymond E., S.S. "How to Read the Resurrection Narratives." *Catholic Update*, March 1996.

———. "Lenten Stories from John's Gospel: Baptismal Dramas of Water, Light and Life." *Catholic Update*, March 1994.

Foley, Leonard, O.F.M. "How the Gospels were Written." *Catholic Update*, May 1983.

Hamma, Robert M. "The Lectionary Heart of the Bible." *Catholic Update*, October 1990 (rev. 1999).

Langenbrunner, Fr. Norman. "How to Understand the Bible: Examining the Tools of Today's Scripture Scholars." *Catholic Update*, March 1982.

McBride, Alfred, O.PRAEM. "The Ten Commandments: Sounds of Love from Sinai." *Catholic Update*, September 1989.

Scott, Macrina, O.S.F. "A Popular Guide to Reading the Bible." *Catholic Update*, December 1984.

Smith, Virginia. "Finding Your Way through the Old Testament." *Catholic Update*, November 1989.

———. "The Whole Bible at a Glance: Its 'Golden Thread' of Meaning." *Catholic Update*, April 1989.

Witherup, Ronald D., S.S. "Acts of the Apostles." *Catholic Update*, April 2007.

———. "Choosing and Using a Bible." *Catholic Update*, July 2004.

———. "Introducing St. Paul the Apostles: His Life and Mission." *Catholic Update*, July 2008.

Contributors

Raymond E. Brown, S.S., was Auburn Distinguished Professor Emeritus of Biblical Studies at Union Theological Seminary and former member of the Roman Pontifical Biblical Commission.

Leonard Foley, O.F.M., priest, popular religious educator, and retreat director, is the author of *Believing in Jesus* and many other books.

Robert M. Hamma is a bestselling author, the editorial director at Ave Maria Press, and editor-in-chief for *Human Development*. He is the author of numerous books and articles on prayer, spirituality, and family life.

Norman Langenbrunner has served as a high-school teacher, associate pastor, and parish pastor. He has written articles for *Liguorian, The Bible Today, St. Anthony Messenger,* and *Catechist.*

Alfred McBride, O.PRAEM., is the author of *Holding Jesus: Reflections on Mary, the Mother of God, The Challenge of the Cross: Praying the Stations,* and *The Story of the Church.*

Macrina Scott, O.S.F., director of Wisdom Center, a ministry of the Marycrest Franciscans in Denver, Colorado, has founded and directed the Catholic Biblical School of the Archdiocese of Denver, and has written many articles and books including, *Picking the 'Right' Bible Study Program,* and *Bible Stories Revisited: Discover Your Story in Luke and Acts.*

Virginia Smith is a writer, editor, and cofounder of *Scripture From Scratch,* a Bible-study program for adult Catholics. She is a retired Catholic educator, working as a director of religious education and chair of the religion department of a Montana Catholic high school.

Ronald D. Witherup, S.S., is provincial of the Sulpician Fathers, former Professor of Sacred Scripture at St. Patrick Seminary, Menlo Park, California, a prolific author, and a frequent contributor to American Catholic Radio. He is the author of *St. Paul: Called to Conversion: A Seven-Day Retreat.*